3/8/22

for
Emmy
the cat
whisperer!
love,
Nana

How to Talk to Your CAT

Jean Craighead George

Illustrated by Paul Meisel

HarperCollinsPublishers

Photographs of Jean Craighead George by Addie Passen

Library of Congress Cataloging-in-Publication Data
George, Jean Craighead, date
    How to talk to your cat / Jean Craighead George ; illustrated by Paul Meisel.
        p.   cm.
    Summary: Describes how cats communicate with people through their behavior and sounds
and explains how to talk back to them using sounds, behavior, and body language.
    ISBN 0-06-027968-0. — ISBN 0-06-027969-9 (lib. bdg.) — ISBN 0-06-000622-6 (pbk.)
    1. Cats—Behavior—Juvenile literature.   2. Human-animal communication—Juvenile literature.
[1. Cats.   2. Human-animal communication.   3. Pets.]   I. Meisel, Paul, ill.   II. Title.
SF445.7.G46   2000   98-41517
636.8'0887—dc21   CIP
                                                                                          AC

❖

To Sam

—J.C.G.

For Sally and Harriett

with thanks

—P.M.

You are being honored
if a cat is living with you.
Cats are loners. They don't like company.
They don't even like the company of
another cat. They hunt by themselves.
They are completely self-sufficient
and can leave you at any time
and go off and make a living. And yet
cats can have warm and loving
relationships with humans.

What explains this contradiction?

The cat.

Humans did not domesticate the house cat as they did the dog. The cat domesticated itself. About 4000 B.C. the Egyptians began storing their wheat and rice in granaries. Mice settled in and ate the grain, and the wild Kaffir cat, *Felis sylvestris*, stole in from the desert and ate the mice. This wild cat slept by day and hunted by night. It caught fish and birds as well as mice, and it slipped into and out of homes with silent dignity. The Egyptians were charmed by its talents and beauty. They not only encouraged it to become a household pet, but they eventually elevated it to the rank of a goddess, the goddess Bast. Goddess or not, the cat remained wild. Just like wild animals today, the young of the wild Kaffir cats were friendly to humans but turned against them when they grew up.

Around the year 2000 B.C. a slightly different species appeared among the wild Kaffir cats. It had shorter legs and a narrower head, but more important, it was as sweet as a kitten to humans even as an adult. *Felis catus*, the domestic house cat, had evolved. It purred, flattered humans with its silky touches, and wooed them with cat talk.

What is this cat talk?

Cat talk is a complicated, self-centered language. If you speak to your cat first, it probably won't speak back. Cats initiate conversations. To understand them, you have to feel, look, listen, and even smell. Cat talk is scent, touch, sound. It is movements of tail, ears, whiskers, and the pupils of the eyes. It is body language. It is enchantment.

There is no best age to learn language from a cat, and there is no best age to take one home. Kittens, adolescents, and adults all adjust quickly

to life on beds, pillows, sunny windowsills, and warm fireplaces, and to cat snacks. There is one thing to know about cats: The cat that picks you, the one that meows at your door asking to be taken in, makes the best pet. You have not forced yourself upon it. Of its own free will it has chosen you. That's what a cat is all about—free will.

Take only one cat. Cats are solitary animals. They dislike other cats and will fight at a whisker twist. If you want two cats, get them when they are kittens, preferably from the same litter. They will spar and tumble, but not wage war. They might even purr to each other and sleep side by side. Older cats brought together will occasionally work out a truce with each other but need space and time to do so.

Among cats, "Hello" is rubbing heads. When your cat rubs its head on your leg or arm, it is saying hello to you. Most people will be moved to pick it up. That is an answer, but it is not a cat "hello." To answer the greeting, get down on your hands and knees and rub heads with your cat. It will probably reply by arching its back and raising its tail. Whiskers will cup forward to embrace you. This ballet is a big "hello."

You might be able to initiate a cat conversation by staying away for the day. When you return home, you'll probably get the "I missed you" talk. The cat runs to you. The fur is pressed lightly to the body with whiskers bowed forward. The pupils are large with pleasure, and the tail is held straight up like a flagpole. Sometimes the cat adds, "You've been gone a long long time," by rising on its hind legs and arching its shoulder and neck toward your hand. Stroke its head to say, "I'm glad to see you, too."

There is no such thing as a cat "good-bye." They do not need it. When you walk off, they go their independent way with no sulking. Only when you come back do they have something to say.

You and your cat are speaking in scent when you exchange touches.

A cat touch is silent talk. Scent glands lie along the flank and the lip, under the chin, on the top of the head, and along the tail of the cat. When you are rubbed by flank, lip, chin, head, or tail, you are being told, "You are my property."

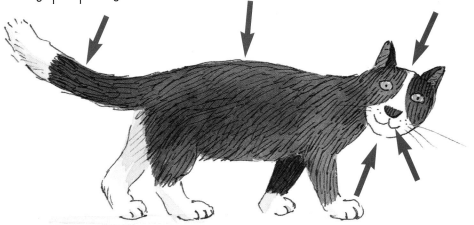

Although you can't smell the message, you will probably answer by picking up or petting your cat. Now you have scent marked the fur. However, you have not said, "You are my property." You have said, "Yes, I am your property." That's cat talk. They own you. You cannot own a cat. Isn't it interesting that we license dogs to claim our ownership, but not cats?

The cat uses the sound *meow* to speak of its needs to humans.
Individual cats have worked out as many as nineteen different *meows* to get their points across. Your part in the meow conversation is to do what is being asked of you.

MEOW!—This is the command sound. The cat wants attention or a deed performed.

If given near the door, your cat is telling you to let it go outside. The tail often has a crick in it.

Your cat talk: Open the door.

If given near the food bowl while weaving around your feet and with the pupils of the eyes small, the cat is asking you for food.

Your cat talk: Open the cat food and feed the cat.

Listen to your cat's meows. You'll hear the difference between "Let me outside" and "Feed me, I'm starved."

mee-o-ow (starting high and dropping)—This is a protest. Your cat has not gotten what it wanted. It is whining.

Your cat talk: Give the cat more food or more attention. Pick it up. Smooth the fur.

MEE-o-ow —Same sound only louder. This is a strong protest. You haven't figured out what it wants.

MYUP!—Given sharply. It's the meow contracted into one note. You have stepped on its tail, removed its favorite pillow, not understood what it is saying, and it is myuping in righteous indignation.

MERRRROW!—This is the cat's swear word. It is given quickly and loudly, the ROW cut short.

Your answer: Get out of the way.

mier-r-r-r-ow (chirped and with a cadence)—This is a loving expression of intimacy. You are being told you are the most beloved piece of property in your cat's domain.

This needs no answer. Enjoy your high status.

RR-YOWWW-EEOW-RR-YOWOW—This blood-curdling sound is the caterwaul given by the tomcat calling to a mate at night.

Your defense: Put a pillow over your head and go back to sleep.

In addition to the variations on the meow, there is hissing and spitting. The lips are curled, canines exposed. This is the cat warning signal, usually directed at other cats or a dog.

Some cats think you are telling them you are going to attack when you walk straight at them. This is how they tell another cat they are out for blood. Tell them you are not going to leap on them by coming toward them from the side or at a diagonal. Nice cats approach their friends in this manner.

The purr distinguishes the cat from all other animals. No other animal can make such a sound. Never having heard it before, even a child knows that it says, "I'm content and happy." It is an audible smile; it is luscious satisfaction and the witchery through which cats charm people.

No one knows how the purr is made or what part of the anatomy it comes from. The cat can purr while breathing in and breathing out.

There are several kinds of purrs. The normal smoothly running purr means the cat has been moderately pleased by your petting it or the comfort of your lap. The three-part down-up-down purr announces that the cat is more than just comfortable, it is divinely content. This purr is often so loud, it can be heard across a room.

Amazingly, the purr is never given when the cat is alone. Sitting in the sun on a soft pillow will not turn on the purr; curled on the hearth before a toasty fire won't do it either. The purr is communication, and cats are too smart to talk to themselves.

It is possible for you to begin a purr talk by sitting down and making a lap. You may have to wait a long time, but eventually the lure works.

The cat will decide when it has had enough and jump to the floor. If you try to hold it back, you'll hear tough cat talk. This is made up of the purr-snarl, claws out, whiskers bowed back, and tail whipping. The cat is saying, "Don't restrain me . . . or else." Wise people let their cat depart.

14

You, however, can end the purr session by standing up. The cat jumps to the floor with a loud thump of its feet—foot talk—which says, "I don't like this." A cat can land on its feet without making a sound, so listen for feet. You will know you have talked to your cat.

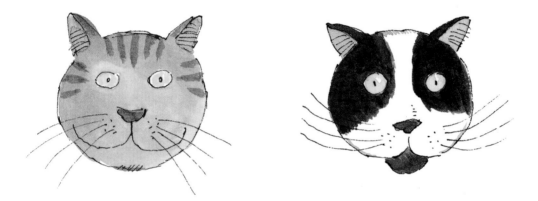

Moving whiskers are also cat communication. Bent forward, they mean the cat is enclosing you, loving you. Bent backward, the cat is saying it is alarmed. It has thrust its whiskers out of the way to bite.

Watch whiskers. If they are forward, you can hug the cat. If back, get out of the way.

Also watch the tail, the silent communicator.

The cat is very honest. Its tail tells you just how it feels.

The tail held straight up says, "I like you."

When it is hanging down and loose from the body, the cat is saying, "All is well."

Straight up but bent over at the tip means "I am not so sure of you."

Put one arm straight above your head to tell the cat you like it.

When the fur at the base of the tail stands up, the word is "I am worried." This is usually about dogs or another cat in the vicinity.

The famous Halloween-cat pose—back arched high, fur standing up all over the body—is cat war talk. It is on the defensive, but it is also ready to attack. "I'm afraid, but watch out—I'm dangerous."

A lashing tail is anger.

The tail of a cat can say, "I'm humble." The legs are flexed; the tail is arched out from the body and curved upward at the tip like a dipping spoon.

This is rare talk. A cat is seldom humble.

The cat's face, like its tail, also talks to you in silence. Read what it is saying. You can reply when you know what is being said.

When the ears are up and forward, the head tilted slightly downward, and the lower eyelids lifted, your cat is saying, "I like you." Its face is soft and loving.

Most people speak back to this face without knowing they're doing it. They pick up the cat and caress it. The "I like you" is hard to resist.

Here is some more facial talk:

"Someone is coming."—Ears up, eyes wide, pupils narrow. Lips and whiskers are relaxed. It's probably a dog. If a cat is coming, the ears twist back until their openings are to the side.

 "I'm alarmed."—The openings of the ears are down, the pupils small and in the center of the eyes.

 "I'm going to attack."—Ears up, openings to the side, pupils enlarging.

 "I'll swat!"—Ears straight out from head and down; pupils are pinpoints.

 "I'll bite."—Ears flat out and openings down. Mouth open to expose canine teeth.

 "Here I come!"—Ears plastered to the head and back. Mouth wide open. Pupils almost filling the eyes.

Cats also send messages with their legs.

Scraping the ground with the back feet says, "Scram. Get out of here, or else I'll fight."

You can tell a cat to scram by scraping your feet while turned sideways to it. This is often more effective on stranger cats than saying, "Shoo." Why? The back legs deliver power messages. The legs are used for vaulting after prey and, in a fight, for tearing open the belly of an opponent. No cat takes back-leg messages lightly.

Front legs speak, too. Tearing at the upholstery with the front legs and claws is the cat way of saying, "I am powerful. I am sharpening my weapons. Beware." The cat is peeling off the outer covers of its claws, honing them to a lethal point. The deeper the claws dig, the more status the cat has.

There are a few ways to speak to a cat first.

Cats are passionate hunters. Tie a string to a piece of paper, drop it to the floor, and jerk it along like a mouse dashing for shelter. Then let it lie still. The cat talk begins.

The tail will twitch to say, "That mouse is mine!" Pull the paper. Your cat will pounce. If it gets the paper, its tail goes up and curls over the back. "Got the mouse!" it is saying.

You can also make a bird. Swing the paper on the string just above your cat's head. It will leap and clap its paws together. "Gotcha." Again the tail goes up and over the back. "Victory!"

To talk fish talk, put your cat on top of a counter—if it lets you—and dangle the paper below. A paw swings down in a scooping motion to say, "I am fishing."

Some cats will "talk hunt" with the reflected light from a mirror or with the spot from a flashlight. They leap, spring, turn, and pounce, displaying all the beauty and grace of the cat.

As all people who are owned by cats know, cats have a way of sitting right where you are reading or writing. Words will not shoo them away. Neither will pushing or dropping them to the floor. They will be back. The best way to tell a cat to get off your book is to arouse deep cat instincts.

Put a brown paper bag on the floor. Now place your cat beside the bag. The cat is gone. The bag is throbbing. The cat is exploring, testing, settling down. Cats HAVE to go into caves and holes—and paper bags and boxes. You have told your cat to leave you alone. You are free to read for quite a while.

Now that you know the ABCs of how the cat talks through its senses and body language, you are ready to read its secret language.

Within each human home the cat constructs an orderly town. Instead of restaurants, spas, salons, hotels, and verandas, the cat has food spots, sunning spots, grooming spots, sleeping spots, and lookouts. These are connected by scented pathways. If furniture is moved in the way, the cat will go over it, down, and continue on.

Observe the pathways and see why this solitary, independent animal has a loving relationship with humans. Through its secret language of scent it marks out a luxurious world within your world. Sleeping spots are the softest beds or pillows, lookouts are warm windowsills above a radiator or heater. Food, water, and kitty litter are available. Cats love luxury providers.

Outside your house your cat marks off a more natural and wilder town. Hunting spots are under bird feeders, and around trash cans and junk piles where mice live. Sunning spots and lookouts are in trees or on the tops of low buildings. Pathways lead to mates. No other cat dares come down these pathways.

If one does, your cat will sit, tuck its feet under its chest, and pull in its neck. The intruder does the same. They both stare at each other and then away. They repeat this over and over again until the intruder leaves or they fight.

A cat fight is a ritual. While the female sits regally, her front feet tucked neatly under, two male rivals approach each other, heads high, tails twitching. Insults are given. Cat insults are the sniffing of noses, flanks, and anal areas. This is usually followed by sitting and more staring, in the hope that staring will drive one or the other away. If not, one biffs the other's face with a forepaw and rolls underneath him. This is the cat's offensive position. Here he can rake the opponent's throat with unsheathed claws. The big hind legs can rip the belly.

Blood-curdling screams will fill the night.

The one on top runs off. Both may be bleeding. Cats will nick but not kill each other.

At dawn each cat returns to its outdoor grooming spot, bloody but unbowed. They clean their whiskers, paws, and fur. They doctor ears and check nicks. They eventually MEOW to come into your house, or if privileged enter by way of the cat door. Each will walk its path to its favorite bed.

This is probably right near or on your head. Although you will be awakened and even annoyed, you should be flattered. You have been talking good cat talk. Your cat did not have to come home at all.